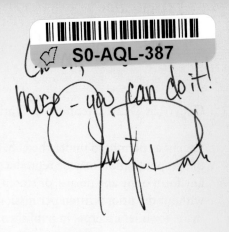
Baby Traveling Tips

for

The Clueless Chick™

Sourced Media Books, LLC
20 Via Cristobal
San Clemente, CA 92673
www.sourcedmediabooks.com

ISBN–13: 978–1–937458–08–9

LCCN: 2012910463

Printed in the United States of America.

This publication is designed to provide entertainment value and is
sold with the understanding that the publisher is not engaged in
rendering legal, accounting, or other professional advice of any kind.
If legal advice or other expert assistance is required, the services of a
competent professional person should be sought.

—From a Declaration of Principles jointly adopted by a
Committee of the American Bar Association and a
Committee of Publishers and Associations

Baby Traveling Tips

for

The Clueless Chick™

Jennifer Durbin

Sourced Media Books, LLC
San Clemente, CA

To Jenny, for your constant support, enthusiasm, and inspiration.
To Carmel, for being the best advisor a Chick could ask for.

Contents

Foreword

Baby Traveling Tips for The Clueless Chick™ is the second in a series of pocket guides for the professional woman who would spend hours upon hours planning and reviewing websites if she had more than five minutes to spare in her busy day. Written by the quintessential Type-A/OCD overachiever, The Clueless Chick™ is a collection of pocket guides for navigating through the milestones and obstacles all women, girlfriends, wives, and mothers face. First and foremost, I do not claim to be an expert traveler, although I have traveled a good bit with both of my little ones. What I am is a woman just like you, albeit a little obsessed with overresearching life's little challenges, and I'd like to share what I've learned from my experiences (and mistakes). My hope is that I will be able to save you hours of research and days of searching hundreds of websites in your quest for the one kernel of knowledge you are looking for. Baby Traveling Tips for The Clueless Chick™ will afford you the time to focus on the fun part of planning your trip and avoid some of the common pitfalls of poor planning. When you are finished with this pocket guide, you will feel less "clueless"—armed with a roadmap to follow wherever the road may take you.

Welcoming a baby into your life is very exciting. Congratulations! Chances are you spent months preparing and planning for the arrival of your little one, but you probably didn't give too much thought to where he was going to sleep when you went to Grandma's house for Thanksgiving or how you were going to get him a passport for international travel.

Baby Traveling Tips for The Clueless Chick™ is a compilation of everything I wish I had known before I ever left the house with our first son. You can think of this as a quick-start guide for getting out and on with your lives based on all of the research I have done over the years. My advice comes straight from my experiences, the experiences of my friends, and the countless magazines, websites, and blogs I have studied in my never-ending effort to make traveling with little ones as painless as possible. Having traveled as much as possible with my husband before we had children, it was very important to me that we continued to travel as a family. I have always strived to expose my little ones to new experiences, and the best way to do that is to experience the rest of the world.

Whether you are terrified to spend the day at the zoo with your little one or ready to start racking up frequent flyer miles, this is the book for you! I'll walk you through all of the major steps of traveling with a little one, from packing a diaper bag to making a hotel room feel like home to obtaining a passport. This guide will be here for you to refer back to whenever your plans call for travel. No matter where you are going or how you are going to get there, I am here to clue you in!

1

Diaper Bags

Diaper bags do not have to be yet another "necessary evil" of motherhood—have fun with it! Yes, you have to carry a diaper bag, but no, it does not have to be an old fuddy-duddy teddy bear and clown bag (unless that's what you're into). Think of a diaper bag as yet another fun accessory! Remember how fun it was picking out all of those adorable little baby clothes and cool toys? This is your chance to pick out something just for you! Yes, the purpose of the bag is to carry all of the little one's paraphernalia; however, it is also your chance to make a fashion statement. In those first few weeks after baby is born, when you're sleep deprived and feeling gross, and in those next few (or many) months, when you feel like you'll never get your body back, don't underestimate the power of a fun accessory! If you pick the right diaper bag, there will honestly be times when you will look forward to going out just so you can carry yours!

As with anything, diaper bags come in every price range. You may choose to pick up a $5 bag at a local thrift shop or drop $2,500 on the new Louis Vuitton diaper bag. Your diaper bag will quickly become your main accessory for a few months, so it may be worth it to splurge on a nice bag in lieu of getting a new purse. So set your budget, and let's start shopping!

Diaper Bag Styles

Diaper bags come in every style imaginable, so you're likely to find just what you are looking for if you do a little digging. If your local stores don't carry exactly what you want, do some hunting online. The downside of purchasing a diaper bag online is that you can't "try it on for size"; and, given that this will be a nearly constant accessory, you'll want to love it! Make sure you are familiar with the return and exchange policy of wherever you purchase from.

When picking out a diaper bag, remember that you may want to have more than one. After all, you may not want to take your primary diaper bag with you to a baseball game, where you want to carry as little as possible and be able to toss it under your seat. You also want to keep in mind that a diaper bag is simply a very large purse for the baby. So think of your favorite large purse or shoulder bag and consider picking a diaper bag in a similar style.

There are six main types of diaper bags available in just about every color and price range imaginable. Here are the main features and benefits of each type:

1. Classic Diaper Bags

- Often come with a removable longer strap so they can be worn across your body.

- Have one or many outside pockets for easy access to small items.

2. Messenger/Across-the-Body Bags

- Easily worn over the shoulder or across the body.
- Designed to be less bulky than a traditional diaper bag.

3. Stroller Bags

- Meant to hang over your stroller handlebars.
- Caution: Be mindful of your stroller manufacturer's recommendations about stroller bags, since some lighter-weight strollers may become unstable with the added weight of a diaper bag on the handlebars.

4. Backpack

- Great for hands-free outings.
- Usually not "too girly" for Dad and can hold just about everything.

5. Nontraditional/Laptop Bag

- A lot of diaper bags, especially designer diaper bags, can easily be used as laptop or carry-on bags after they have served their original purpose.
- The reverse is also true; a laptop bag can meet all of your diaper bag needs!

6. Diaper Bag for Dad

- Diaper Dude makes great "dad-friendly" diaper bags, which are usually messenger bags.
- This can be a fun surprise for Dad!

Where to Find a Diaper Bag

Online

- www.zappos.com
- www.diaperbags.com
- www.poshtots.com
- www.ebags.com
- www.fleurville.com
- www.DiaperDude.com
- www.SkipHop.com
- www.jjcolecollections.com
- www.babiesrus.com
- www.buybuybaby.com
- www.etsy.com

Brick-and-Mortar Stores

- The store where you registered for baby gifts
- Big-box stores (Target, Wal-Mart, etc.)
- Maternity boutiques
- Anywhere that carries baby stuff
- Department stores
- Your favorite designer purse store

Like any baby product, it is a good idea to read reviews on diaper bags and get other moms' opinions before you start shopping. You may even find that a mom's negative review of a bag is all the information you need to decide that it is the perfect bag for you. Some of the best places to find diaper bag reviews are:

- www.babygizmo.com
- www.consumerreports.org
- Your favorite blog
- *Baby Bargains: Secrets to Saving 20% to 50% on Baby Furniture, Gear, Clothes, Toys, Maternity Wear, and Much, Much More!* by Denise Fields

If you don't find a traditional diaper bag that fits your style, needs, or budget, try one of these inexpensive alternatives:

- Buy a beach bag, laptop bag, or large purse.
- Check your local thrift store or consignment shop.
- Use a large bag that you already have!
- If you can sew, make your own!

If you are still having trouble, just grab an old bag from the back of your closet and use it for a while—that will give you time to figure out exactly what you like or need.

Which Diaper Bag Is Best for You?

Questions to ask yourself when choosing a diaper bag:

❑ Does this diaper bag fit my style?

❑ Will this be my main/only diaper bag?

❑ Will this diaper bag hold everything I need?

❑ Can I easily access everything I need? Are there enough compartments and small pockets for bottles, diapers, toys, etc.?

❑ Will Dad also carry this diaper bag? (This may rule out the super cute pink floral bag.)

❑ Is this diaper bag comfortable to carry?

❑ Does this diaper bag fit under/on my stroller?

❑ Will this diaper bag hold up to spills and being tossed in and out of the car/stroller/etc.?

❑ Can I afford this diaper bag?

Packing Your Diaper Bag

You will be carrying a lot of things in your diaper bag, many of which are small. Your diaper bag may have countless built-in pockets, which is great, but there may be times when you need to grab only what you need and go. Or you may want the ability to switch from one bag to another quickly. For instance, I always want to be able to quickly grab a diaper, changing pad, and wipes for a quick diaper change. If your little one uses a pacifier, you will want to know that you can easily reach into your diaper bag without looking and grab one (one of the many skills you instantly acquire once you have a child).

Is One Diaper Bag Enough?

Is one of anything ever enough? While you can definitely get by with one diaper bag, you'll find that you really need at least two different bags based upon where you are going and how long you will be gone. Having two or three diaper bags can save time and headaches. After all, you don't want to fumble through your "Big Bertha" diaper bag at the grocery store, and you don't want to throw your Coach diaper bag under a football stadium seat.

Ideally, you should have three different diaper bags to meet all of your on-the-go needs. You'll need the following:

- Small "grab-and-go" diaper bag for the basics.
- Large "full-size" diaper bag for day trips and traveling.
- Mid-size "backup bag" that can be tossed under a seat.

Having multiple diaper bags does not mean spending a mint. Here are some easy ways you can spend little to no money on your second and third diaper bags:

- Use the free bag you got from the hospital or formula company.
- Try a larger purse or laptop bag that is sitting in the back of your closet.
- Borrow from a friend.
- Pick one up at your local thrift store.

Note: This section may be used to prove to your partner that you need to buy three designer diaper bags. But keep in mind that you can easily get everything you need in three high-quality diaper bags for under $100.

What to Take, When

Think of packing your diaper bag like packing a suitcase. You wouldn't pack the same for an overnight trip as you would for a week at the beach, would you? The same holds true for your little one. You do not need to lug as much stuff to the grocery store as you need to pack for a day at the zoo. You also do not need to have everything within arm's reach at all times. For example, if you are at a friend's house for the day, you can simply bring in your "grab-and-go" while leaving all of your day trip items in the car—if it is easy enough to run out to the car and grab what you need, don't weigh yourself down. But how do you know what to take, when? Follow these simple guidelines, and packing your diaper bag will be a snap. (Note: No matter where you are going, make sure you always have emergency items, such as medications, with you.)

Everything you will ever need to throw into your diaper bag can be broken down into four categories. You may even find that you are able to eliminate a few of these items as your little one gets older or if you are comfortable improvising:

1. Basics: Everything you need to get by. The basics can easily fit into your "grab-and-go" bag for quick trips (errands around town, the grocery store, a play date, etc.).

2. "Mommy must-haves": To eliminate the need for a separate purse, simply throw your "mommy must-haves" into the diaper bag. It is easiest to put most of these items into a wristlet that you can simply throw into whichever diaper bag you are taking with you.

3. Eating on the go/outings: These items are for eating out

at a restaurant or for going on an extended outing (afternoon at the park, trip to the doctor's office, etc.).

4. Day trip/overnight: The items in this category are for long trips like the zoo, an outdoor festival, a night at Grandma's, a week at the beach, etc.

What to Pack in a Diaper Bag

Basics

☐ Diapering
- Diapers (at least two)
- Wipes
- Changing pad
- Diaper cream
- Scented diaper baggie or zip-top bag for dirty diapers/soiled clothes/trash

☐ Feeding
- Nursing cover
- Formula in premeasured container, bottle, water
- Snack
- Burp cloth

☐ Health and safety
- Medication
- Hand sanitizer
- Tissues
- Pacifier/teething ring

☐ Clothes and entertainment
- Change of clothes (appropriate for the current season)
- Toys/crayons/book/puzzle

Mommy Must-Haves

- ❑ Phone
- ❑ Wallet/cash
- ❑ Feminine products/nursing pads
- ❑ Water bottle (especially if you are still nursing)
- ❑ Anything else you cannot live without (lip balm!)

Eating on the Go/Outings

- ❑ Basics
- ❑ Mommy must-haves
- ❑ Cleansing
  - High chair cover
  - Table topper
  - Zip-top bag for trash
- ❑ Feeding
  - Cooler with homemade baby food or jars of food
  - Fork/Spoon
  - Bib
  - Snacks (bananas, puffs, rice cakes, cereal bars, crackers, applesauce)
  - Snack containers: snack traps, reusable baggies, cleaned baby food containers, formula dispensers

Day Trip/Overnight

- ❑ Basics
- ❑ Mommy must-haves

- ❏ Eating on the go/outings
- ❏ Extras: Diapers, wipes, formula, bottles, snacks, clothes
- ❏ Meals
- ❏ Sunscreen
- ❏ Lovie/music box for nap time and bedtime
- ❏ Head-to-toe body wash for a quick bath

Diaper Bag Space-Saving Tips

Pack This	Not That
Receiving blanket	Blanket Nursing cover Changing pad
Sanitary wipes	High chair/cart cover Table topper Hand sanitizer
Bib clips*	Bibs
Smartphone apps	Toys Books

*These are just like the alligator clips the dentist uses to hold the paper around your neck and can turn a cloth or paper napkin into a bib. They come in countless shapes and colors and can range in price from $5 – $20. They are also super easy to make (or ask your dentist for one!) but not as stylish or adjustable.

Organizing Your Diaper Bag

Now that you've laid out everything you will need to pack in your diaper bag, let's talk about organization. The key to staying organized is having a place for everything and putting everything in its place. Knowing what's in your diaper bag will save you time and frustration when you're running out the door and make it so you can reach into the bag later with one hand, without looking, and grab whatever you need. It will also make asking someone to grab the formula out of the diaper bag much easier if you can say, "Grab the formula that is in the front right pocket in a green container."

There are numerous storage containers and systems specially designed for baby items or diaper bags. While these are great organization solutions, you may be able to find very inexpensive or even free alternatives:

❑ Free cosmetic cases: Save the gift with purchase cases you've collected from your favorite makeup counter to carry all of baby's small needs (nail clippers, brush, travel body wash, etc.). Note: they are also perfect for all of your electronics (iPod, chargers, camera, etc.).

❑ Zipper/snap/Velcro top vinyl bags: Save the vinyl bags that pillow cases and toys come in to carry a couple of diapers, wipes, and a changing pad.

❑ Ziploc bags: Great for carrying a few wipes if you don't have a reusable container or for transporting dirty diapers, soiled clothes, or trash.

❑ Reusable sandwich bags: Perfect for feeding accessories, snacks, or toys.

❑ Small bottles with tops: Small bottles with resealable tops, such as the free breast milk containers you get at the hospital, are perfect for snacks, small items, or homemade shakers.

❑ Drawstring gift bag: Ideal for smaller toys so they do not roll around at the bottom of the diaper bag.

Diaper Bag Must-Haves

Diapers

- Carry a few scented diaper disposal bags or a zip-top plastic bag in case you're changing the little one in a spot that was not set up for diaper disposal. If you are at a friend's house, she will greatly appreciate this.

Wipes

- Have enough for diaper changes, quick hand cleaning, and spills.

- Use a refillable travel wipe container to save money.

Changing Pad

- Pack a cloth, vinyl, or disposable changing pad. You will want to put something—anything—between your baby and a public restroom changing table. You'll also want to protect your girlfriend's $200 bedspread from a messy diaper. Personally, I love disposable changing pads because they are compact and sturdy enough to be used many, many times.

- In a pinch, you can also use a small blanket or your nursing cover.

2

Leaving the House

Traveling with an infant, whether across town or across the state, can seem like a very daunting task—but it doesn't have to be tough! A little planning and some strategic packing will make for a much easier trip. The most important thing to remember is to relax; there is nothing that will stress out the baby more than if you are tense. When it comes to leaving the house with baby, the three most important logistical considerations are:

- Timing
- Destination
- Season

By taking into consideration the logistics involved in leaving the house with your little one, you can take most of the stress out of the experience. If you have no qualms about leaving the house, fantastic! If, on the other hand, you are the mom who literally takes her baby nowhere but to the pediatrician's office in the first four months of his life, here are a few tips to get you out the door and on with your lives! Remember that it is just as important that your little one become comfortable being in public as it is that you continue to have a life.

Logistical Considerations

Before you take your newborn out in public, it is important to consult your pediatrician about when it is safe to expose your little one to strangers' germs. When you are thinking about going out with your little one, you want to take three things into consideration:

Timing

- When do you need to arrive at your destination?
- How long do you need to stay?
- When do you need to be home?
- Will you need to feed the baby while you are out?

Destination

- Are you already familiar with the destination?
- Is the destination stroller-friendly?
- Will noise levels, crowds, or cleanliness be an issue?
- Do you have an exit strategy if you need to leave quickly?

Season

- Will you need to take additional warm clothes?
- Will you need warm-weather accessories?
- Is it likely to rain/snow?

Once you have determined what your challenges on this outing may be, it will be much easier to plan for them. As long as you have the necessary basic supplies, there is nothing to worry about. If on the off-chance things go sideways, you can always pack up and leave.

When to Leave

Deciding on the best time to leave the house may very well be the key to a successful outing. Whether you are running to the grocery store, keeping a doctor's appointment, or heading out for the day, the timing of your departure can be pivotal. Planning around your little one's schedule can make for a much easier day. For example, if you leave right before nap time only to discover that your little one will not nap in the infant carrier, you may be in for a LONG trip. If, however, you leave right after mealtime or nap time, you will have a perfect little angel to show off. The most important part of this equation is knowing your little one's habits and disposition so that you can optimize his good moods and be home in time to handle the tougher times of the day.

If you have no choice but to leave during a nonideal time of the day, it is very important that you have what you need to make the little one as comfortable as possible—especially if you are going to try to sneak in a nap. It is not a bad idea to be flexible with your little one's schedule once in a while, but you may have a readjustment period ahead of you.

Taking an Overnight Trip

Taking your little one out of town for an overnight trip, or leaving your child with a sitter for a night or two can seem a bit daunting. Will you remember everything? What will you do if you forget something? How will you keep your little one entertained without all of those cool gadgets you have at home?

These are all very valid concerns. The good news is that with the right amount of preparation and know-how, you can be prepared for just about anything. Depending on your mode of transportation, your preparations will vary slightly.

It is important to prepare for your travels as much as you can so that you are not in a rush the day you plan to leave or scrambling to find a critical item you forgot. This does not have to mean hours and hours of prep work. In fact, if you spend too much time preparing, you may be too tired to enjoy the trip or too stressed-out to roll with any unexpected occurrences.

Tips for Working up to Your First Big Outing with Baby

❑ Take baby steps. Take a long walk around your neighborhood or to a local store or restaurant.

❑ Take advantage of how easy it is to transport a little one in an infant carrier—they won't always sit still.

❑ Pick a kid-friendly spot to visit. The first time you eat out with a little one who is not simply sleeping in the infant carrier, try a casual/noisy restaurant where people may not notice a little fussing.

❑ Find a local movie theater that has a kid-friendly movie showing, where they turn down the volume and turn up the lights.

❑ Join a local mommy-and-me or meet-up group.

❑ Schedule a dry run of a long trip. Spend the day at a friend or neighbor's house, or use a movie theater to simulate an airplane.

Tips for a Successful Overnight Trip

❑ Plan to buy bulky items such as diapers, wipes, formula, food, etc. at your destination so you have less to carry.

❑ Compile a list of urgent cares, doctors, pharmacies, etc. at your destination, just in case. If you are taking an extended trip, or if your child has special medical needs, ask your pediatrician for a local point of contact.

❑ If you are concerned about local water (too hard near the coast, etc.), use bottled water.

❑ If you can, schedule your departure time during the little one's "good" time of the day when he is less likely to be fussy.

❑ Do your best to keep the little one on her normal schedule so that your trip and your transition back to normal when you arrive home go as smoothly as possible.

❑ Don't be surprised if the trip home is harder because the little one has been off her normal schedule while you were away, and you are all tired.

❑ Most importantly, enjoy the trip! Don't forget that most people are very understanding. As long as you are doing what you can to keep the baby comfortable and quiet, you'll be fine. You likely won't ever see these people again, anyway.

Planes, Trains, and Buses

When you will be traveling in a confined space, there is definitely a balance between packing just enough and too much. You want to have everything you need, but you don't want to pack too much. Lugging everything on and off of the plane—with the baby—can be tough.

Think back to when you first packed a diaper bag. You probably started by throwing in everything you thought you might possibly need. Then, after a few outings, you pulled half of the stuff out. Think of prepping for a trip with baby in the same way. You need emergency medicine and supplies to be able to diaper, clothe, and feed your little one. The rest in your bag will make life easier.

Before You Fly

- Let the airline know you are traveling with an infant/ toddler under age two. Some will add "infant in arms" to your boarding pass, while others will issue a separate no-seat boarding pass for the little one.

- Read all of the airline's policies regarding traveling with a child.

- Travel with a copy of the baby's birth certificate for identification purposes.

- Read all of the TSA guidelines for traveling with children to ensure that your trip through airport security goes smoothly.

- Consider taking your little one in for a checkup and asking your pediatrician any questions you may have.

Packing for a Flight

When you fly, you will need to pack both a suitcase and a carry-on for your little one. Gone are the days when you could simply hop on a plane with nothing but your purse. Consider packing your carry-on just like packing your diaper bag, only on a larger scale. When you are flying, you do not have the luxury of stopping at the nearest drugstore to pick up more diaper cream, so it is important to pack what you will need. Your checked luggage, on the other hand, will not be accessible until you reach your destination—so don't put your backup diapers there!

What to Keep with You

Diaper Bag

❑ Bring your day trip/overnight diaper bag. (Take advantage of every space-saver tip you can!)

❑ Pacifiers are great for helping little ones' ears pop during takeoff/landing or calming them during a fit.

❑ Nursing covers/blankets are perfect to cover an over-stimulated baby for nap time.

❑ Plenty of sanitary wipes—you might want to clean something/everything she is going to touch.

❑ Extra zip-top bags for trash, soiled clothes, or dirty diapers will come in handy.

❑ Tylenol is important, just in case the little one develops a fever or is suffering from teething pain.

❑ A nose bulb is needed, so you can clear his stuffy nose.

❑ Extra clothes are useful in case you are diverted, lose your luggage, or miss your flight.

❑ Extra diapers and wipes are all-important, because you just never know . . .

❑ A surprise toy if things get rough can change night to day.

Equipment

❑ A lightweight stroller that reclines for toddlers or an infant carrier and stroller frame will save tired feet.

❑ Gate check bags for stroller and car seat/infant carrier are a must; you really don't want the stroller or car seat banging against all of the dirty things under the plane!

❑ A Baby Bjorn/baby carrier helps keep your hands free if you are not taking the infant carrier on the plane.

Things to Pack in Your Checked Luggage

❑ Formula

❑ Diapers

❑ Wipes

❑ Bottles/sippy cups

❑ Bottle brush and soap

❑ Spoons and bowl

❑ Music-maker for nap and bedtime

❑ Cooler for homemade baby food with ice pack

❑ Bumbo for play time, feeding, and bath (if you are super careful)

❑ Booster seat (preferably one that straps to a chair)

❑ Monitor (either your nice one, or a cheap one from a consignment store)

❑ Clothes

❑ Toys

Once you have determined what you'll be taking with you, it is important to plan your activities so that you are not caught without any idea of how you are going to entertain your little one. This is particularly important because you will be spending most of your trip in a very confined space and may be stuck at an airport for hours between flights or due to delays.

At the Airport

- Getting through security can be a challenge because you are carrying a lot of stuff! Many airports have a special line for families, so pay attention to which line you are getting into. Make sure you remove all liquids from your bags, and let the security officer know which bags contain items for the baby, such as premixed formula or liquid foods.

- If you are traveling with an infant or toddler under the age of two and did not purchase an extra seat for her, sweet-talk the gate agent into putting you next to an open seat, if one is available, so you can take the car seat on board for the little one. The little one will be much more comfortable if she has room to move, and so will you.

- Buy bottled water when you get past security to mix formula on the plane or fill the little one's sippy cup.

- If you are stuck at an airport between flights, take advantage of the space in the terminal (or consider camping out in an adjacent terminal to take full advantage of the opportunity) to stretch out or burn off some energy. Let the little one run around an empty gate area. Find an empty gate and have him take a nap. Put down a blanket and have a picnic. Or just roll around and play.

- Change your little one's diaper as close to boarding time as reasonable to avoid the discomfort of a dirty diaper and to minimize the number of diaper changes on the plane.

On the Plane

- Feed the baby at takeoff and landing to prevent her ears from building up too much pressure. Give your toddler a chewy snack to help pop her ears.

- Make friends with the people sitting around you on the plane as soon as you can—just in case.

- A change of scenery can do wonders—when the baby gets fussy, take a walk to the back of the plane or let her check out the bathroom.

- Most importantly, *relax.* If you are tense and stressed-out, your little one will not relax.

- Put toys/snacks in an unexpected container that your little one can play with. My toddler once spent fifteen minutes putting Cheerios into a formula dispenser and then using it as a shaker.

- Take a pack of Post-it flags for your toddler to stick all over the seat, pull off, and stick on again. Large Post-it notes are great for drawing on the tray table.

- Take a special snack that your child does not eat regularly as a surprise.

- Talk to your toddler about everything that is going on to keep him interested/distracted.

- Load movies or cartoons on your smartphone or tablet for in-flight entertainment. Make sure to test your movies the night before and have headsets ready to go if you plan to use them.

When You Arrive

- Let the little one stretch and run around to burn off pent-up energy.

- Get your little one back on normal schedule as soon as possible to make your trip go more smoothly.

- Immediately unpack any necessities so that you are not rushing to find something in the middle of the night.

Car Trips

Preparing for a car trip is similar to preparing for any other overnight trip, except you usually have the added luxury of space and do not have to "pack" everything, since you can simply throw larger items into the trunk or backseat. You will, however, want to resist the temptation to take anything and everything just because you can.

Before You Drive

- If you've never taken a road trip with a little one, buckle up—you're in for a heck of a ride. Once you've mapped out your driving route, it is a good idea to plan your stops. While you will likely need to make an unscheduled stop or two, you can save yourself time and stress by mapping out scheduled stops based on feeding/meal schedules.

- Before you hit the road, check your tire pressure, fluid levels, etc. (see www.aaa.com), and empty out any unneeded items. You will also want to ensure that your emergency kit is fully stocked with baby necessities.

Baby Emergency Car Kit

❑ Seasonal items
  - Winter—blanket, warm clothes, warm hat, etc.
  - Summer—extra water, light clothes, hat, sunscreen, etc.

❑ Baby bottle

❑ Formula

❑ Baby food

❑ Water

❑ Snacks

❑ Diapers

❑ Wipes

Packing for a Car Trip

Packing for a car trip is very similar to packing for a flight—you want to have the necessities within arm's reach, and everything else can go in the trunk. In a pinch, you can simply pull over and grab what you need out of the trunk, but don't underestimate how much time a few quick stops can add to a trip. The potential downside of having extra space is the temptation to put everything in a number of small bags that fit behind and in between seats. While this may be ideal for the drive, it will leave you with fifty bags to carry in when you arrive at your destination.

Things to Consider When Packing for a Car Trip

❑ Everything you put into the car you will have to carry in to your destination.

❑ Having all of the necessities within arm's reach will eliminate frustration and unscheduled stops.

❑ Expect the unexpected—pack emergency supplies for the current season.

What to Pack for a Car Trip

- ❏ Entertainment

- ❏ A personal DVD player (if you do not have an entertainment system) and DVDs

- ❏ Kid-friendly music

- ❏ A list of fun car games (i.e., I Spy)

- ❏ Snacks that won't make a mess or leave little ones with sticky hands (i.e., crackers that crumble)

- ❏ A portable potty if traveling with a potty-trained toddler

---

Tips for a Successful Car Trip

- If you have good sleepers, leave at bedtime. Once the little one is in his PJs, buckle up!

- If things get stressful, pull over and walk around.

- Sit in back with the little one for a while.

- If it is a really long drive, feed on the go. Clearly, you can't nurse on the go, but you can feed the little one a bottle if you're in the back seat.

- Have diaper and wipes handy to grab and jump out of the car for a quick change.

- Have a mirror in the back if the little one is in a rear-facing car seat.

Accommodations

While you are traveling, you will be staying either with friends and family or in a hotel/motel or rental property. Both types of accommodations come with their own pros and cons. For some, staying with family and friends can feel just as comfortable as being at home, while for others the thought of staying in someone else's house is a nightmare. Whether your accommodations are ideal or not, good planning will make everything easier (where have I heard that before?).

Choosing a Hotel or Rental Property

Before You Leave

- Confirm your reservation, and reserve a crib and mini-fridge if it does not come standard with your room.

- Many hotels will simply give you a Pack 'n Play so you can bring your own sheet if you like. I am personally not a fan of the full Pack 'n Play covers some hotels supply, because they never fit right.

- Bring a night-light for the corner of the room the baby is sleeping in.

- If you plan to let your little one crawl around the room, consider packing a few outlet covers or tape.

- Bring something to do while the baby is asleep. If you will all be in the same room, you may not want to have the TV blaring while the little one is sleeping.

When You Arrive

- Place your luggage in front of the door to ensure little hands do not open it. While hotel door locks do a great job of keeping people out, they automatically unlock when the handle is turned from the inside.

- Take full advantage of the continental breakfast, and grab a banana or a box of cereal for a snack. Juice cups are also the perfect size for little hands to play with or to use as snack containers.

- If there is no continental breakfast, make sure you have morning snacks with you so you don't have to rush out to get food in the morning.

- Eating in the hotel room can be easy if you use the stroller as a makeshift high chair.

- If you are fortunate enough to have a kitchenette in your room, take full advantage and stock up on snacks and meals.

When You Leave

- Check every nook and cranny to make sure little hands didn't hide something important. Pay particular attention to drawers and trash cans.

Staying with Friends and Family

Staying with friends and family will usually give you much of the flexibility you have at home in terms of cooking, space, and creature comforts. If your host has children, you may be able to borrow much or all of the gear you need, which will save you the hassle of traveling with it. If the host has no baby gear, you may be able to borrow key pieces from a friend or rent from a local store.

Although your host may be understanding if you have a fussy little one or are still getting up for middle-of-the-night feedings, it is important to be a good house guest. Many people will recommend that you do whatever you can to comfort your little one, even if it means backsliding on things like weaning off of a pacifier or making the baby sleep in his own bed. Do keep in mind that when you get home, there may be an adjustment period to get back on your normal schedule.

Renting a Car

If you are renting a car at your destination, consider also renting a car seat. This is an easy way to eliminate the need to lug a car seat with you. Renting a car seat will also allow you to avoid the wear and tear on your car seat that can result from sliding and banging around in the plane cargo hold. Most rental car companies regularly inspect car seats to ensure that they are still safe. However, there is no telling where the car seat was last, so bring sanitary wipes.

3

Eating on the Go/Eating Out

Going out to dinner or eating on the go while traveling does not have to be a challenge. But—you guessed it—some planning is required. While you are still transporting your little one everywhere in an infant carrier and he is sleeping through just about everything, go out to eat as much as possible! Once he starts to move and groove, meals will be a lot quicker and potentially trickier.

What to Feed Your Little One at a Restaurant

- Instead of ordering a separate meal for the little one, let her eat part of your meal.

- Carry shelf-stable organic milk in your diaper bag, in case the restaurant does not have milk.

- Look for a restaurant that serves you a basket of bread when you sit down. It is a super-easy snack for the little one that will keep her busy.

- Carry a few backup snacks (applesauce, rice cakes, cereal bars, Cheerios, Goldfish crackers, etc.).

Restaurant Logistics

- As soon as you sit down, clear everything off the table that little hands can reach and put down your table topper.

- If you are ordering a meal for the little one, order as soon as you sit down or have a snack ready.

- Be mindful of the people sitting around you. If the little one becomes too disruptive, take him on a short walk.

- Ask for the check as soon as your food arrives, just in case you need to make a quick exit.

- Take advantage of crayons offered for little ones. They can be a good distraction, and you can keep them in your diaper bag for next time.

- Always ask for extra napkins, just in case.

- Clean up any mess your little one has made.

- In a pinch, use a teaspoon instead of toddler silverware, bread or fresh fruit instead of snacks, sanitary wipes instead of a table topper, and The Clueless Chick's straw trick instead of a sippy cup (see text box on opposite page).

If You Are at a Restaurant That Does Not Usually Serve Children ...

- Use your stroller as a high chair or carry a small booster seat with you.

- Ask for water in a to-go cup for the little one.

- Order a kid-friendly appetizer or share your meal.

- When all else fails, use The Clueless Chick™ straw trick to give the little one some of your water: Put your straw into a glass of water, cover the top of the straw with your finger while holding your finger on the top of the straw, remove the straw from the water, and place the straw in your little one's mouth. Release your finger and let your little one drink the water. Be careful not to release your finger too quickly and overwhelm her with too much water!

Nursing on the Go

If your little one is still nursing, feeding her on the go can be much easier but may still require a bit of planning. First, you should never leave home without your favorite nursing cover. If you are comfortable nursing anywhere at any time, have at it. If, however, you are more on the modest side, there are usually more private spots you can find:

- A store dressing room

- The back seat of your car (weather permitting)—with a DVD playing, if you've got one!

- An empty gate at the airport
- A nice bench or picnic table at the park
- The coat check room at a restaurant or event space
- An office in a store at the mall
- A bathroom (if you absolutely have to)—with a chair you can set up in a corner

Traveling with Homemade Baby Food

If you are making all of your own baby food (good for you!), don't worry—it is not hard to travel with homemade baby food. It will, however, take additional time to prepare everything that is needed to travel with homemade baby food. You will also need a game plan for if you run out of food. Will you make food? Will you buy jar food? Above all else, remember that it is not the end of the world if you have to feed your little one jar baby food while you are away from home. I was once an hour from the house when I realized that I had left the cooler with the baby's dinner in it on the kitchen counter. So I broke down and swung by a local grocery store and picked up a jar of organic sweet potatoes and a jar of organic peas. Yes, this was the only jar food he ever ate, and I never again left the house without my cooler.

Before You Leave

- Plan your menu and prepare all food in travel containers such as Baby Cubes for easy transport and storage.
- Label everything very well. When flying I always place a large "Homemade Baby Food" label on the outside of any food in my checked bag, in case TSA decides to take a peek.

- Travel with frozen food so it is less likely to spoil in transit. Only thaw the food she will need within the first few hours of your trip.

- Pack food in a small cooler that freezes in the freezer (these coolers stay cool forever).

- Pack extra food in your carry-on, just in case your flight is delayed or canceled or your little one hits a surprise growth spurt.

- Pack supplies such as your favorite dish soap and brush to clean your food containers and utensils.

- Pack an immersion blender for puréeing food on the go (it isn't any bigger than a hairdryer).

- Decide what food you will purchase and prepare at your destination.

- Research where the local grocery stores are.

- Call your hotel and ask them to set up a mini-fridge in your room.

While You Are Traveling

- Place frozen food in the fridge before you go to bed to let it thaw overnight.

- Warm cold food by placing it in a small cup of hot water.

- Purchase food that is easy to "smash and serve" with nothing more than a fork: fresh fruit (bananas, pears, melon, etc.); bread, crackers, or rice cakes; or cooked carrots, canned pears, or applesauce.

- Have a separate baggie to throw empty food containers into.

4

Traveling Without Your Baby

If you travel for work, or you and your partner finally get a chance to sneak away for a couple of days, leaving baby at home can be stress-free with the right preparations and planning. While prep work won't help you miss baby any less, it will help you worry less.

In additional to preparing your own things for your trip, you will need to do the same for your little one who is staying at home. If your little one will not be staying at home but with a family member or sitter, simply follow the "Traveling with Baby" instructions for packing his things. On the other hand, if the baby will be at home, it is nice to leave out everything the caregiver will need to dress and care for the little one.

There are two important lists you need to make before leaving your little one: what to leave with the babysitter and what to take with you.

Tips for Traveling Without Baby

What to Leave with the Babysitter

❏ Daily instructions

- Feeding
- Sleeping
- Activities
- Transportation options

❏ Emergency contact info

- Pediatrician
- Local hospital
- Poison control
- Your number and destination
- Neighbors
- Friends (Have a trusted adult on call in case the caregiver has questions.)
- Medical insurance card and release form

What to Take with You

❏ Sitter's contact information
❏ All emergency contact info
❏ Copies of vital records
❏ Recent pictures of the little one

Traveling Without the Baby While You Are Still Nursing

Traveling with a baby can be a trick, and traveling without the baby when you are still nursing can be even more of a trick. First, there is the obvious—you will miss the little one like crazy! Second, you have to figure out what to do with all of the breast milk you will produce while you are away from your baby.

You'll obviously need to pack a pump and all of the accessories. It can be easier to pump into storage bags, since they take up less space. Just be sure they are completely sealed. As a backup, you can slip all of the full storage bags into a gallon-size zip-top bag.

Just like you would call your hotel to request a crib and fridge for the baby stuff, call them and ask for a fridge to store your milk. For storage in transit, take a small cooler with you.

Pumping on the Go

If you will need to pump on the go (and if you're traveling, you have to), you will have to jump through some logistical hoops.

- Invest in an electric travel pump if you are going to be traveling a lot. If it is a short trip, you can get away with a manual pump (much cheaper, and you don't need batteries or a plug), but plan to spend a good bit of time pumping.

- Always carry batteries, in case you cannot find a plug.

- You cannot live without a hands-free bustier that will keep both pumps in place at once so that you can read, type, etc. For a low-cost alternative, you can buy a cheap sports bra that clasps either in the front or back, and cut a nickel-size hole in the nipple area.

Milk Storage and Transport

- Breast milk can be stored at room temperature for a number of hours—some say up to ten hours.

- A large to-go cup with a lid half-filled with ice is perfect for storing a couple of full bags of breast milk.

- Most major shipping companies will have a way for you to overnight milk on dry ice, but be prepared to pay a good bit.

- For going through security, check the current TSA regulations for traveling with breast milk. It is very important to know your rights; you may even want to print a copy of the current regulations to refer to. Most importantly, notify the TSA agent that you are carrying breast milk before you put your belongings on the X-ray belt. That way, there will be no surprises.

Pumping at an Airport

Scope out the airports on your route when you're booking travel. Simply Google "pumping at LAX," for instance, and you will find great resources that include blogs by other traveling mothers. If the airport doesn't have a nursing room or family restroom, see if there is vacant office space, or buy a pass to one of the airline clubs. If all else fails, you can find an outlet at an empty gate and use your nursing cover to cover yourself.

5

Leaving the Country

Whether you're an old pro at international travel or are taking your first international trip with baby in tow, you need to plan ahead. Not only do you need to allow four to six weeks to obtain a passport for the little one (after you have spent hours preparing the application package and appearing in person with the little one and your partner), you will have to do your homework about your destination(s). We take for granted that domestically you can usually find a Target, Wal-Mart, etc., if you need to grab extra diapers or a can of formula. But what do you do when you are in a foreign country and cannot read the label on a jar of baby food? The key to surviving (and enjoying!) an international trip with baby is planning, planning, and more planning.

Obtaining a Passport

Before your little one can leave the country, she must have a passport, no matter her age. If you've traveled internationally before, you know what a pain it can be to obtain or renew your passport. Think of the process of getting your passport, then add twenty additional hoops to jump through. If you give yourself enough time (at least two to three months) to complete the process, it does not need to be stressful. You will, however, need to be mindful that this is a process that will most likely require that you take time off work, so plan accordingly when you are allocating your vacation days.

The State Department has broken the process for obtaining a passport for a minor into nine simple steps with no less than twenty-three substeps. It is very important that you read through all of the steps and instructions carefully, so as to not delay the process. There are companies that, for a fee, will manage the passport request process for you. Also, know that if at all possible, BOTH parents will be required to appear in person with the little one at a passport agency or acceptance facility (such as a U.S. Post Office).

Passport Basics

- Visit the State Department website and read all of the instructions to apply for a passport for minors (http://travel.state.gov/passport/get/minors/minors_834.html).

- Complete all of the required steps and paperwork.

- Make an appointment at your local passport agency or acceptance facility to submit all of the required paperwork and photos.

- Wait four to six weeks (two to three weeks if expedited) for the little one's passport to arrive.

- Have a fantastic trip!

You will also find that it is not inexpensive to obtain a passport, so budget accordingly. In 2012, the cost to obtain a passport book (not card) for a minor was $105, and if you need the passport expedited, it is an additional $60. The good news is that a minor's passport is good for five years. The bad news is that if the little one is still under the age of sixteen when his passport comes up for renewal, the renewal process and cost is the same.

Before you book your international travel, remember:

- You cannot apply for a passport until your little one has a Social Security Number.

- Passport processing takes four to six weeks, once the entire passport package is submitted (two to three weeks if you pay an additional fee to expedite).

- Follow all form instructions to the letter to ensure that you do not inadvertently delay the processing or waste a trip to the passport agency.

- Both parents and the child should be present to sign and submit the passport package, if at all possible. If you are a single parent, or if for whatever reason the other parent is physically unable to appear in person, there are additional forms and processes you must go through.

- Passport packages can be submitted at either a passport agency or acceptance facility such as a Post Office. Most locations require appointments; and, even if they don't require appointments, it can save a good deal of time if you make an appointment. There is almost nothing worse than being stuck in a long line with baby in tow.

- Take special care to read all payment instructions, as some fees may need to be paid separately and the facility where you are submitting your passport package may not accept credit cards or personal checks.

Preparing to Travel Internationally

If you have the good fortune to be traveling to see family and friends internationally, you may not need to do any more prep work than you would for a domestic trip. If, however, you will not have a resource locally while you are overseas, it is important to do your homework prior to hopping on a plane.

While this may sound like a daunting task, it may be as easy as spending a couple of hours online. For example, a Google search for "traveling to Spain with a baby" will give you a number of different blogs and local resources to read. It can be extremely helpful to read someone else's horror story or favorite tips before you embark on your adventure!

Shopping for Baby Necessities Internationally

Unlike traveling domestically, you may not be able to pop into the local Target to buy an extra can of Similac formula when you are in the French countryside. So it is important to know what the comparable local brands are, especially if your child is sensitive or has any allergies. Make sure you have a translated list of everything your little one is allergic to, so you can ask a local resident for help, if necessary.

It is helpful to know what brands you will find at the local grocery store before you arrive (many may look familiar). If you aren't able to find this information before you leave, make sure you have a good translation dictionary for reading labels. If all else fails, ask the store manager, a pharmacist, or (even better) a local mom for help.

For more general tips about traveling internationally (not specifically traveling with a baby), refer to:

- www.fodors.com

- www.tripadvisor.com

- www.frommers.com

- www.ricksteves.com

These sites can tell you where to obtain local currency, whether you will have any trouble using your credit cards or smartphones, etc. They can also tell you what types of power adapters to take and how to find the best translation dictionary or app for your smartphone. Be sure to also speak to your pediatrician before you leave, since he or she can be another tremendous resource.

6

Travel Safety Tips

Whether you are traveling domestically or internationally for two days or two months, it is always important to travel safely. You may feel like you've always been a safe traveler, but now you need to make special considerations for your little one. For instance, if your child is under age three, she may not be able to tell a stranger her name if you two are separated. It can also be challenging to prove a child's identity, so it is important to plan accordingly.

Safety Tips

- Carry a current picture of your little one and a copy of his birth certificate.

- Put an ID on your little one, such as a SafetyTat or ID wristband. Sites like www.safetytat.com and www.mypreciouskid.com can facilitate this.

- Make a list of important numbers, such as the local urgent care center, for where you are staying and for home.

- Enroll in the STEP program if you are traveling abroad.

- Be sure to travel with any medication your little one may require, and consider also carrying a copy of the actual prescription.

International Travel Safety Tips

The State Department's website (www.state.gov) is a fantastic resource for information about international travel, travel warnings and alerts, etc. They also offer the option to enroll in STEP (Smart Traveler Enrollment Program) to receive automated updates and alert the local consulate of your presence in that country, should there be an emergency.

Be sure to know what type of international medical coverage you have and travel with all of the necessary documentation (ID card, etc.). If your child has a medical condition, be sure to alert your pediatrician of your travel plans and arrange to carry a sufficient amount of medication with you. You will also want to ensure that your child is appropriately vaccinated for foreign travel. Simply search the CDC's website (www.cdc.gov/travel) for your destination(s), and you will see a wealth of information pertaining to local health concerns and recommended vaccinations.

Know who to contact locally in case of an emergency. For instance, in much of Europe you can dial 112 to reach local ambulance, fire, and police services (and 999 in England). However, in some parts of the world, you need to dial the local services directly, since there is not a universal emergency number.

7

Travel Gear

In addition to all of the little things you will be throwing into your diaper bag/suitcase/carry-on, there are a few larger travel gear items that you should consider packing. The number of items you take will depend on how old your little one is, where you will be traveling, and how long you will be there. For instance, it may not be worth packing an infant travel swing if you are going on a two-night trip to the beach, but it will be worth its weight in gold if you are flying to Granny's for a week.

Must-Have Travel Gear

- Lightweight stroller (preferably one that reclines) or an infant carrier stroller frame

- Baby carrier (front carrier or backpack) for travel to locations that are not stroller-friendly, or if you plan to do hiking, etc.

- Gate check bags if you are flying with a car seat or stroller

- Travel swing or infant carrier swing frame

- Bumbo (great for playtime, feeding, or bathing—just be super careful)

- Booster seat (preferably collapsible with straps to attach to a chair)

- Infant travel bed or PeaPod

- Travel Lite crib/Pack 'n Play (Travel Lite is simply a mini-Pack 'n Play)

- Travel potty seat or disposable potty, if toilet training

Travel gear can be expensive. Before you purchase any, do your homework. Ask friends, search for reviews online, and refer to our favorite gear experts:

- *Baby Bargains: Secrets to Saving 20% to 50% on Baby Furniture, Gear, Clothes, Toys, Maternity Wear, and Much, Much More!* by Denise Fields

- www.babygizmo.com

- www.consumerreports.org

- Your favorite blog or friends' tips on travel gear

Ways to Save Money on Travel Gear

- Rent gear at your destination (www.babytravelpros. com).

- Borrow from a friend.

- Shop your local consignment store or craigslist.org. Many people only use their travel gear for one trip, so you can usually find items in very good condition.

- Leave the booster seat at home and use the stroller as a high chair.

- Repurpose items from around the house. For instance, use a large, black trash bag with your phone number on a piece of masking tape in lieu of a gate check bag.

8

Other Great Resources

There is no such thing as being too prepared or having too much information before you travel. But there are only twenty-four hours in the day, and there is such a thing as wasting time worrying about irrelevant details. So do a little reading, talk to a few experienced friends, and hit the Web!

Here are a few of my favorite travel blogs and websites:

- www.deliciousbaby.com
- www.travelswithbaby.com/blog
- www.havebabywilltravel.com

I hope this book has saved you many hours of research and has armed you with the traveling tips you need to feel comfortable taking your little one anywhere. I also hope you feel less "clueless" about traveling with your little one. With this guide at your side, you are ready to tackle everything that traveling with your little one can throw your way! While there is a lot of planning involved, just pace yourself and enjoy the experience. You'll handle it all easily!

To keep up with the latest travel trends, gear, and tips, visit *www.CluelessChick.com.* There are also almost literally a million different blogs you can follow that contain helpful information and insights—or simply make you laugh. It is important to remember that blogs, like many things, are one person's unfiltered opinion. And you know what they say about opinions!

Now, go put all of your newfound knowledge to work! It is time to do a little planning and a lot of packing. Whether you're trying to pack a diaper bag for a picnic in the park or hopping a plane to Beijing, start stocking up on the necessities and get packing! Just remember to relax and enjoy every minute of your adventure.

For the latest tips and information about The Clueless Chick™, visit our website, *www.CluelessChick.com.* I hope you will keep coming back for more tips!

Until next time,

Jennifer

Origins of The Clueless Chick™

On June 30, 2009, my husband, Matt, and I were settling in for the night after putting our six-month-old to bed. Matt was telling me about another one of his brilliant book ideas, and I was only half paying attention. As he went on and on, it hit me that I needed to write a book! After all, I had just created a blog to collect all of my tips and tricks that people had been asking me to send them for years. If so many of my friends (and friends of friends) were interested in what I had to say, maybe I was on to something. The idea for The Clueless Chick™ series was born!

Matt and I immediately started brainstorming ideas and quickly determined that I would write a new series as a "contemporary CliffsNotes for the modern woman." I would help every woman, girlfriend, wife, and mother who would spend hours researching about all of life's milestones and obstacles—if she had more than five minutes to spare in her busy day. As the quintessential Type-A/OCD overachiever, I can share all of my tips, tricks, and research to help point you in the right direction on your journey. I am here to clue you in!

Tear It Out and Take It with You!

Which Diaper Bag Is Best for You?

Questions to ask yourself when choosing a diaper bag:

❑ Does this diaper bag fit my style?

❑ Will this be my main/only diaper bag?

❑ Will this diaper bag hold everything I need?

❑ Can I easily access everything I need? Are there enough compartments and small pockets for bottles, diapers, toys, etc.?

❑ Will Dad also carry this diaper bag? (This may rule out the super cute pink floral bag.)

❑ Is this diaper bag comfortable to carry for hours on end?

❑ Does this diaper bag fit under/on your stroller?

❑ Will this diaper bag hold up to spills and being tossed in and out of the car/stroller/etc.?

❑ Can I afford this diaper bag?

Diaper Bag Space-Saving Tips

Pack This	Not That
Receiving blanket	Blanket
	Nursing cover
	Changing pad
Sanitary wipes	High chair/cart cover
	Table toppers
	Hand sanitizer
Bib clips*	Bibs
Smartphone apps	Toys
	Books

* These are just like the alligator clips the dentist uses to hold the paper around your neck and can turn a cloth or paper napkin into a bib. They come in countless shapes and colors and can range in price from $5 – $20. They are also super easy to make (or ask your dentist for one!) but not as stylish or adjustable.

Diaper Bag Must-Haves

Diapers

- Carry a few scented diaper disposal bags or a zip-top plastic bag in case you're changing the little one in a spot that was not set up for diaper disposal. If you are at a friend's house, she will greatly appreciate this.

Wipes

- Have enough for diaper changes, quick hand cleaning, and spills.

- Use a refillable wipe container to save money.

Changing Pad

- Pack a cloth, vinyl, or disposable changing pad. You will want to put something, anything, between your baby and a public restroom changing table. You'll also want to protect your girlfriend's $200 bedspread from a messy diaper. Personally, I love disposable changing pads because they are compact and sturdy enough to be used many, many times.

- In a pinch you can also use a small blanket or your nursing cover.

Tips for Working up to Your
First Big Outing with Baby

☐ Take baby steps. Take a long walk around your neighborhood or to a local store or restaurant.

☐ Take advantage of how easy it is to transport a little one in an infant carrier, they won't always sit still.

☐ Pick a kid-friendly spot to visit. The first time you eat out with a little one who is not simply sleeping in the infant carrier, try a casual/noisy restaurant where people may not notice a little fussing.

☐ Find a local movie theater that has a kid friendly movie showing where they turn down the volume and turn up the lights.

☐ Join a local mommy-and-me or meet-up group.

☐ Schedule a dry run of a long trip. Spend the day at a friend or neighbor's house. Or use a movie theater to simulate an airplane.

Tips for a Successful Overnight Trip

❑ Plan to buy bulky items such as diapers, wipes, formula, food, etc. at your destination so you have less to carry.

❑ Compile a list of urgent cares, doctors, pharmacies, etc. at your destination, just in case. If you are taking an extended trip, or if your child has special medical needs, ask your pediatrician for a local point of contact.

❑ If you are concerned about local water (too hard near the coast, etc.), use bottled water.

❑ If you can, schedule your departure time during the little one's "good" time of the day when he is less likely to be fussy.

❑ Do your best to keep the little one on her normal schedule so that your trip and your transition back to normal when you arrive home go as smoothly as possible.

❑ Don't be surprised if the trip home is harder because the little one has been off her normal schedule while you were away, and you are all tired.

❑ Most importantly, enjoy the trip! Don't forget that most people are very understanding. As long as you are doing what you can to keep the baby comfortable and quiet, you'll be fine. You likely won't ever see these people again, anyway.

Things to Consider
When Packing for a Car Trip

❑ Everything you put into the car you will have to carry in to your destination.

❑ Having all of the necessities within arm's reach will eliminate frustration and unscheduled stops.

❑ Expect the unexpected—pack emergency supplies for the current season.

Tips for a Successful Car Trip

- If you have good sleepers, leave at bedtime. Once the little one is in his PJs, buckle up!

- When things get stressful, pull over and walk around.

- Sit in back with the little one for a while.

- If it is a really long drive, feed on the go. Clearly, you can't nurse on the go, but you can feed the little one a bottle if you're in the back seat.

- Have diaper and wipes handy to grab and jump out of the car for a quick change.

- Have a mirror in the back seat if the little one is in a rear-facing car seat.

If You Are at a Restaurant
That Does Not Usually Serve Children ...

- Use your stroller as a highchair or carry a small booster seat with you.

- Ask for water in a to-go cup for the little one.

- Order a kid-friendly appetizer or share your meal.

- When all else fails, use The Clueless Chick™'s straw trick to give the little one some of your water: Put your straw into a glass of water, cover the top of the straw with your finger while holding your finger on the top of the straw, remove the straw from the water, and place the straw in your little one's mouth. Release your finger and let your little one drink the water. Be careful not to release your finger too quickly and overwhelm her with too much water!

Tips for Traveling Without Baby

What to Leave with the Babysitter

❑ Daily instructions

- Feeding
- Sleeping
- Activities
- Transportation options

❑ Emergency contact info

- Pediatrician
- Local hospital
- Poison control
- Your number and destination
- Neighbors
- Friends (Have a trusted adult on call in case the caregiver has questions.)
- Medical insurance card and release form

What to Take with You

❑ Sitter's contact information

❑ All emergency contact info

❑ Copies of vital records

❑ Recent pictures of the little one